PIANO • VOCAL • GUITAR

THE SONGS OF
IRVING BERLIN™
PATRIOTIC SONGS

CONTENTS

- 6   Angels Of Mercy *1941*
- 10 Any Bonds Today? *1941*
- 15 For Your Country And My Country *1917*
- 20 Freedom Train, The *1947*
- 24 Gee, I Wish I Was Back In The Army *1954*
- 28 Give Me Your Tired, Your Poor *1949*
- 31 God Bless America *1938*
- 2   How About A Cheer For The Navy *1942*
- 36 I'm Getting Tired So I Can Sleep *1942*
- 58 Miss Liberty *1949*
- 40 Oh! How I Hate To Get Up In The Morning *1918*
- 44 Song Of Freedom *1942*
- 48 This Is A Great Country *1962*
- 52 This Is The Army, Mr. Jones *1942*

Cover Photo: Irving Berlin on stage at the Broadway Theatre, New York, 1942- Performing his famous song "Oh! How I Hate To Get Up In The Morning" in *THIS IS THE ARMY*.

ISBN 0-7935-0382-5

7777 West Bluemound Road P.O. Box 13819 Milwaukee, WI 53213

Copyright © 1991 by the Trustees of The God Bless America Fund and the Estate of Irving Berlin
International Copyright Secured   All Rights Reserved

For all works contained herein:
Unauthorized copying, arranging, adapting, recording or public performance is an infringement of copyright.
Infringers are liable under the law.

Irving Berlin logo is a trademark of The Estate of Irving Berlin
Irving Berlin Music Company is a registered trademark of The Estate of Irving Berlin
GOD BLESS AMERICA™ is a trademark of the Trustees of The God Bless America Fund

ANGELS OF MERCY

Words and Music by
IRVING BERLIN

Moderately

Mer - cy, there's so much to do. The

© Copyright 1941 by Irving Berlin
Copyright Renewed
International Copyright Secured   All Rights Reserved

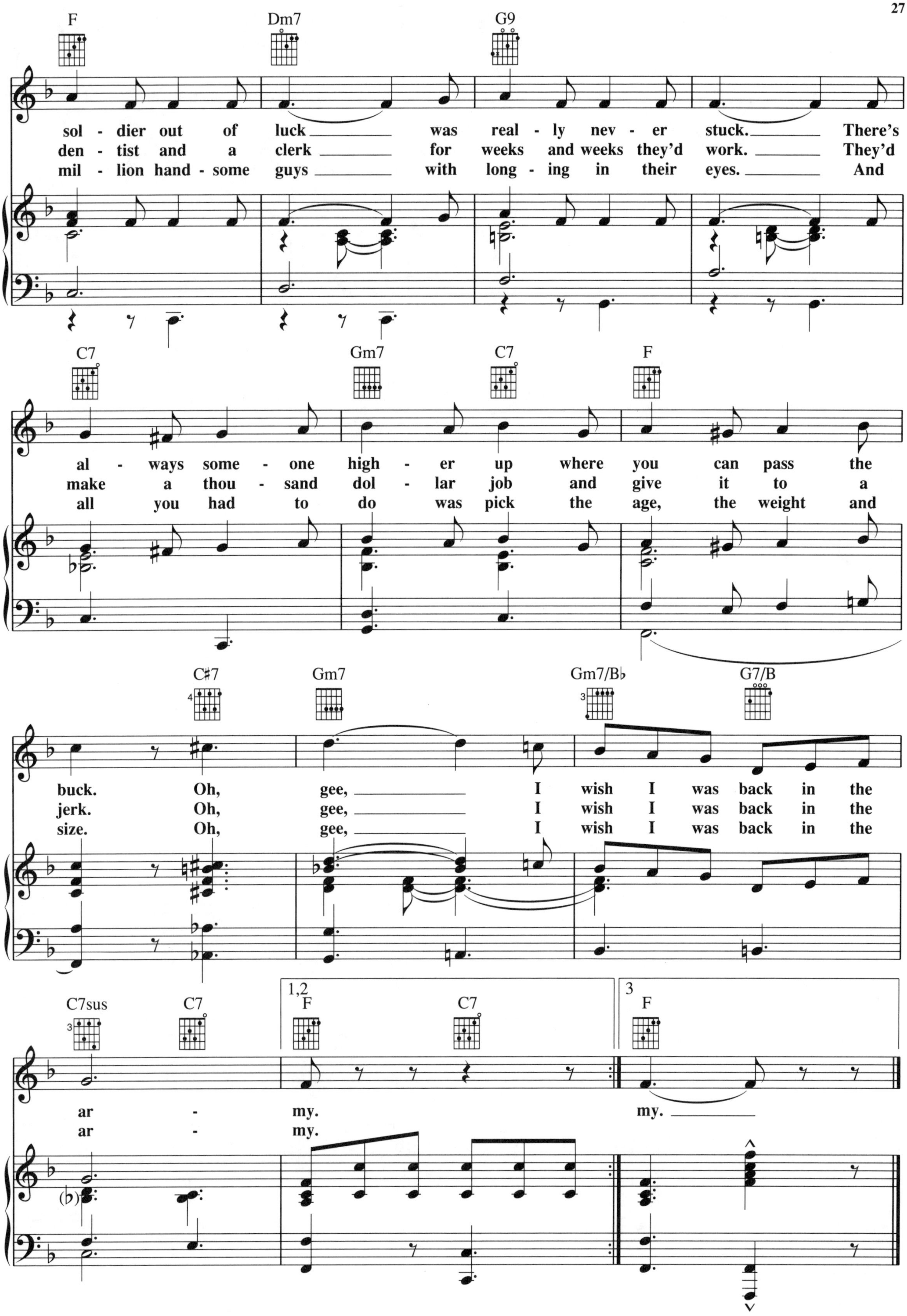
F Dm7 G9
sol - dier out of luck was real - ly nev - er stuck. There's
den - tist and a clerk for weeks and weeks they'd work. They'd
mil - lion hand - some guys with long - ing in their eyes. And
C7 Gm7 C7 F
al - ways some - one high - er up where you can pass the
make a thou - sand dol - lar job and give it to a
all you had to do was pick the age, the weight and
C#7 Gm7 Gm7/B♭ G7/B
buck. Oh, gee, I wish I was back in the
jerk. Oh, gee, I wish I was back in the
size. Oh, gee, I wish I was back in the
C7sus C7 1,2 F C7 3 F
ar - my. my.
ar - my.

getting tired so I can sleep. I want to sleep so I can dream. I want to dream so I can be with you. I've got your picture by my bed. 'Twill soon be placed beneath my head, to keep me com-pa-ny the whole night thru. For a lit-tle while what-ev-er be-falls, I will see you smile till re-veil-le calls. I

E♭
hope you're tired _ e-nough to sleep. And please sleep long _ e-nough to
E♭dim Fm7 B♭7♭9
dream. And look for me _ for I'll be dream - ing
1 E♭ Fm7 E♭ Fm7
too. I'm
2 E♭ Fm7 A♭/B♭ E♭
too.

OH! HOW I HATE TO GET UP IN THE MORNING

Words and Music by
IRVING BERLIN

Moderate march tempo

Vamp till ready

The oth-er day I chanced to meet a sol-dier friend of mine. He'd
A bu-gler in the ar-my is the luck-i-est of men, He

been in camp for sev-'ral weeks and he was look-ing fine. His
wakes the boys at five and then goes back to bed a-gain. He

© Copyright 1918 by Irving Berlin
© Copyright Renewed by Irving Berlin
© Copyright Assigned to Joe DiMaggio, Anne Phipps Sidamon-Eristoff and Theodore R. Jackson as Trustees of God Bless America Fund
International Copyright Secured   All Rights Reserved

muscles had de - vel - oped and his cheeks were ros - y red. ____ I
does - n't have to blow a - gain un - til the af - ter - noon. ____ If

asked him how he liked the life and this is what he said:
ev - 'ry thing goes well with me I'll be a bu - gler soon.

Oh! How I hate to get up in the morn -

ing. Oh! How I'd love to re - main in bed. ____

G G/F E7 Am F7/E♭
For the hard - est blow of all, is to hear the bu - gler
D7
no chord
call; "You've got to get up, you've got to get up, you've
G C/G G Em
got to get up this morn - ing!" Some day I'm go - ing to mur - der the
Oh boy the min - ute the bat - tle is
A9 A7 D7 Am7♭5 D7
bu - gler. Some day they're go - ing to find him
ov - er, oh boy the min - ute the foe is

dead. I'll am-pu-tate his rev-eil-le, and
dead. I'll put my un-i-form a-way, and

step up on it heav-i-ly, and spend the rest of my life in
move to Phil-a-del-phi-a,

bed. bed.

2 Optional 2nd ending to verse 2

bed.

D.S.

SONG OF FREEDOM

Words and Music by
IRVING BERLIN

Free-dom, free-dom, that's my song for to-day. Lis-ten to an A-mer-i-can trou-ba-dor, from the U. S. A. I'm

© Copyright 1942 by Irving Berlin
Copyright Renewed
International Copyright Secured All Rights Reserved

singing a song of freedom, for all people who cry out to be free. Free to sail the seven seas, free to worship as we please. If the birds up in the trees__ can be free, why can't we?___

I'm sing-ing a song__ of free-dom, _____ to all peo-ple where-ev-er__ they may be. _____ Free to speak__ and

D7/A G7 Cm Cm/B♭ D7/A G7
free to hear. _ Free from want _ and free from fear. _
E♭ Cm7 Fm7 B♭7 C Cdim
Sons of free - dom far and near _ who a - gree, sing with me. _
G9 Adim G7
That all God's peo - ple shall be free.
1 C Cdim
Dm7 G7
2 C D♭7 C6/9

THIS IS A GREAT COUNTRY

Words and Music by
IRVING BERLIN

Brightly

Pa-tri-ot-is-m has gone out of fash-ion. We seem to think our pa-tri-ot-ic days are dead. We used to sing of our home-land with pas-sion. But now we

© Copyright 1962 by Irving Berlin
© Copyright Renewed by Irving Berlin
© Copyright Assigned to Joe DiMaggio, Anne Phipps Sidamon-Eristoff and Theodore R. Jackson as Trustees of God Bless America Fund
International Copyright Secured   All Rights Reserved

seem to shy a- way from it in- stead. I think it's time to hit the nail right on the head. This is a great coun- try, a great coun- try. So let's shout it clear and

loud. Take a look in your his-t'ry book and you'll see why we should be proud. Hats off to A-mer-i-ca, the home of the free and the brave._____ If this is flag wav-ing, flag wav-ing, do you know of_____ a bet-ter flag_____ to wave?_____ This is a wave?_____

THIS IS THE ARMY, MR. JONES

Words and Music by
IRVING BERLIN

Brightly

A bunch of fright-ened rook-ies were list-'ening filled with awe. They list-ened while a ser-geant was

© Copyright 1942 by Irving Berlin
© Copyright Renewed by Irving Berlin
© Copyright Assigned to Joe DiMaggio, Anne Phipps Sidamon-Eristoff and Theodore R. Jackson as Trustees of God Bless America Fund
International Copyright Secured   All Rights Reserved

E♭9 A♭ G G7/F
lay - ing down the law. They stood there at at -
C/E G7/D G7 C
ten - tion, their fac - es turn - ing red. The
G G7/F C/E C♯dim Dm7 G7
ser - geant looked them o - ver and this is what he
C7 F B♭
said, "This is the ar - my mis - ter
f

Jones. No private rooms or telephones. You had your breakfast in bed before. But you won't have it there anymore. This is the ar - my mis - ter Green.

We like the bar - racks nice and clean.

You had a house-maid to clean your floor. But she won't help you out an - y - more.

Do what the buglers com-mand. They're in the ar-my and not in a band. This is the ar-my mis-ter Brown.

You and your ba - by went to town. She had you wor - ried, but this is war and she won't wor - ry you an - y - more." more."

MISS LIBERTY

Words and Music by
IRVING BERLIN

Lib - er - ty. _____ The key to the cit - y is

yours. _____ Lib - er - ty, _____ Miss

Lib - er - ty. _____ With ban - ners and stream - ers un -

furled. _____ You're not just the sym - bol of a

To Coda
B♭ Fm/A♭ G7 Cm Cm7♭5 F7 Cm7 F7♭9
stat - ue that we love, but the most beau - ti - ful girl in the
1 B♭ B♭/D Cm7 F7♭5
world.
2 B♭ Cm7 B♭ F7
world. Would you
B♭
like to dine some eve - ning with the As - tors? I'd love to. Would you
F9
like to play a week at To - ny Pas - tor's? I'd love to. Would you

like to come to Trin-i-ty on Sun-day? I'd love to. Would you like to launch a bat-tle-ship on Mon-day? I'd love to. Here's some or-chids fresh with dew from the Pres-i-dent to you. Here's some win-ter flan-nels from the na-tion's moth-ers. Here's some tick-ets for our ball. You'll be wel-come at the hall. Here's some cough drops from the fa-mous beard-ed broth-ers. I re-pre-sent Pratts As-tral Oil, the fin-est ap-pli-ca-tion for a

A♭9 D♭ G♭ D♭/F E♭m A♭7
pim - ple or a boil. We'll pay you hand - some - ly for
D♭ B♭m G♭ A♭7 D♭/F Ddim7
ver - y lit - tle toil. Your pic - ture with a bot - tle of
E♭m7 A♭7 D♭ A♭9 D♭
Pratt's As - tral Oil. I thank you, I thank you, I'm
E♭m7 A♭9 D♭ A♭9 D♭
grate - ful to be sure. Like mon - ey in the bank, you have

made me feel se-cure. Your con-gress, your sen-ate, your pres-i-dent, so dear. But most-ly Mis-ter Ben-nett, the man who brought me here.

D.S. al Coda

CODA

world.